AF078871

FUSS-FREE
4 INGREDIENTS

Editor:
Elizabeth Woodland

LORENZ BOOKS

Contents

Introduction 4

Making Basic Stocks 6

Making Basic Savoury Sauces 8

Juices and Drinks 10

Soups and Appetizers 16

Fish and Shellfish 24

Meat and Poultry 32

Vegetarian, Pasta and Rice 42

Desserts 50

Breads 60

Index 64

Introduction

In recent years, cooking and eating trends have changed considerably, with more emphasis on dishes that are quick and easy to prepare, yet that are still exciting, sophisticated and delicious. This book teaches you how to really make the most of food with simple, fabulous recipes that use only four ingredients, or fewer. Using a limited number of top-quality ingredients allows you to savour the aroma, taste and texture of a dish and saves time on writing lists and shopping for ingredients. It also allows for fuss-free preparation, giving you more time to sit back, relax and enjoy.

Each recipe uses no more than four ingredients, excluding salt, pepper and water. Serving suggestions and ideas for garnishes or decorations are included where appropriate, but these are not essential for the success of the dish. There are also ideas for variations that offer alternative or additional flavourings, and handy cook's tips that will help you achieve successful results every time.

Making Basic Stocks

Good-quality ready-made stocks – either cube, powders or liquid concentrate – are readily available but stocks are easy and cheap to make. Ask for the meat bones when buying from a butcher and trimmings if you have fish prepared by the fishmonger. A good vegetable stock can be made from trimmings. Leave the onion skins on if you want a rich, dark-coloured stock.

Beef Stock

MAKES ABOUT 1 LITRE/1¾ PINTS/4 CUPS

900g/2lb beef bones

2 unpeeled onions, quartered

1 bouquet garni

2 large carrots, roughly chopped

1 Preheat the oven to 220°C/425°F/Gas 7. Put the bones in a roasting pan and roast for 45 minutes, or until well browned.

2 Transfer the roasted bones to a large, heavy pan. Add the onion quarters, leaving the skins on, the bouquet garni and chopped carrots. Add 5ml/1 tsp salt and 5ml/1 tsp black peppercorns. Pour over about 1.7 litres/3 pints/7½ cups cold water and bring just to the boil.

3 Using a slotted spoon, skim off any scum on the surface of the stock. Reduce the heat and partially cover the pan. Simmer on the lowest heat for about 3 hours, then cool slightly.

4 Strain the stock into a large bowl and leave to cool completely. Remove any fat from the surface. Store the stock in the refrigerator for up to 3 days or freeze for up to 6 months.

Chicken Stock

MAKES ABOUT 1 LITRE/1¾ PINTS/4 CUPS

1 large roast chicken carcass

2 unpeeled onions, quartered

3 bay leaves

2 large carrots, roughly chopped

1 Put the chicken carcass and any loose bones and roasting juices into a heavy pan in which they fit snugly. Add the onion quarters, bay leaves and chopped carrots.

2 Add 2.5ml/½ tsp salt and 5ml/1 tsp black peppercorns to the pan, and pour over 1.7 litres/3 pints/7½ cups cold water. Bring just to the boil.

3 Reduce the heat, partially cover the pan and cook on the lowest setting for about 1½ hours. Using a large spoon, carefully turn the chicken in the stock and push down the carcass occasionally.

4 Leave the stock to cool slightly, then strain into a large bowl and leave to cool completely. When cool, remove any fat from the surface. Store the stock in the refrigerator for up to 2 days or freeze for up to 6 months.

Fish Stock

MAKES ABOUT 600ML/1 PINT/2½ CUPS

500g/1¼lb fish bones and trimmings, without heads and gills

1 bouquet garni

1 onion or 3–4 shallots, peeled and quartered

2 celery sticks, roughly chopped

1 Pack the fish bones and trimmings into a pan and add the bouquet garni, quartered onion or shallots and celery.

2 Add 2.5ml/½ tsp salt and 2.5ml/½ tsp peppercorns to the pan and pour over 1 litre/1¾ pints/4 cups water. Bring to the boil.

3 Reduce the heat, partially cover the pan and cook on the lowest setting for about 30 minutes. Leave to cool slightly, strain into a bowl and cool completely. Store in the refrigerator for up to 24 hours or freeze for up to 3 months.

Vegetable Stock

MAKES ABOUT 1 LITRE/1¾ PINTS/4 CUPS

3 onions, quartered

200g/7oz mushrooms

300–400g/11–14oz vegetables, such as broccoli, carrots, celery, tomatoes and leeks, roughly chopped

45ml/3 tbsp green or brown lentils

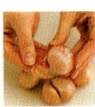

1 Place the onions in a heavy pan with the mushrooms, mixed vegetables and green or brown lentils.

2 Add 2.5ml/½ tsp salt, 10ml/2 tsp peppercorns and 1.7 litres/3 pints/7½ cups water to the pan. Bring to the boil, then reduce the heat and simmer, partially covered, for 50–60 minutes.

3 Leave the stock to cool slightly, then strain into a bowl and leave to cool. Store in the refrigerator for up to 24 hours or freeze for up to 6 months.

Bouquet Garni

This little bundle of herbs is perfect for adding flavour to stocks, soups and stews and is easy to remove after cooking. A traditional bouquet garni comprises sprigs of parsley, thyme and a bay leaf, but you can vary the herbs according to the dish and/or main ingredients.

1 Using a short length of string, tie together a bay leaf and sprigs of thyme and parsley.

2 Alternatively, place the herbs in the centre of a square of muslin (cheesecloth) and tie into a neat bundle using a short length of string.

3 Use the bouquet garni straight away or freeze. Herbs tied in muslin are better suited to freezing than bundles simply tied with string.

FREEZING STOCK

Stock freezes very well. Once it has been strained and the fat removed, reduce the volume by boiling the stock uncovered. This concentrates its flavour and takes up less freezer space. A highly reduced stock, boiled to a thick syrup, can be frozen in an ice cube tray. Make a note of the volume before boiling, then add this to the label when packing the stock for the freezer. This way you will know how much water to add when the concentrated stock is thawed.

Making Basic Savoury Sauces

A good sauce can provide the finishing touch to a dish. One of the most basic is the classic savoury white sauce, which can be served as a simple topping for vegetables or flavoured with additional ingredients. A basic fresh tomato sauce is widely used for pasta dishes, pizza toppings and vegetable dishes. It can be stored in the refrigerator for several days or frozen for up to 6 months. Hollandaise sauce is another classic accompaniment for fish and vegetables. Unlike the other sauces it cannot be made ahead, but it is commercially available.

White Sauce

MAKES ABOUT 300ML/½ PINT/1¼ CUPS

300ml/½pint/1¼ cups milk

15g/½oz/1 tbsp butter

15g/½oz plain (all-purpose) flour

freshly grated nutmeg

1 Warm the milk in a small pan. In a separate pan, melt the butter over a gently heat, then add the flour and cook, stirring, for 1 minute until the mixture forms a thick paste.

2 Remove the pan from the heat and gradually add the warmed milk, whisking continuously until smooth.

3 Return the pan to a gentle heat and cook, whisking, until the sauce boils, is smooth and thickened. Season with salt and freshly ground pepper and plenty of nutmeg.

Fresh Tomato Sauce

MAKES ABOUT 1 LITRE/1¾ PINTS/4 CUPS

1.3kg/3lb ripe tomatoes

120ml/4fl oz/½ cup garlic-infused olive oil

1 large onion, finely chopped

small handful of basil leaves, torn, or 30ml/2 tbsp chopped fresh oregano

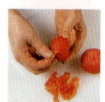

1 Put the tomatoes in a bowl, pour over boiling water to cover and leave to stand for about 1 minute until the skins split. Drain and peel, then roughly chop the flesh.

2 Heat half the oil in a large pan. Add the onion and cook gently for about 3 minutes until soft but not browned. Add the tomatoes the remaining oil.

3 Add the herbs to the pan, cover and cook gently for 20–25 minutes, stirring frequently, until the sauce is thickened and pulpy. Season to taste.

> **VARIATIONS**
>
> • Try using herbs such as marjoram, thyme or rosemary in place of the basil or oregano.
>
> • To make a mildly peppery sauce add a little paprika, for a spicy sauce, add a little chilli powder.
>
> • To make a much more garlicky sauce, add 2–3 crushed garlic cloves to the softened onions.

Hollandaise Sauce

MAKES ABOUT 120ML/4FL OZ/½ CUP

45ml/3 tbsp white wine or herb-infused vinegar

1 bay leaf

2 egg yolks

115g/4oz butter, chilled

1 Put the vinegar in a small pan with the bay leaf and 5ml/1 tsp black peppercorns. Boil until reduced to 15ml/1 tsp, then strain into a heatproof bowl.

2 Put the vinegar in a clean pan, add the egg yolks and a little salt and whisk lightly until thoroughly combined. Cut the chilled butter into small pieces.

3 Add the butter to the pan and set over a very low heat. Whisk continuously so that as the butter melts it is blended into the egg yolks. When all the butter has melted, continue whisking until the sauce is thick.

4 Season the sauce with salt and ground black pepper to taste, adding a few extra drops of vinegar, if you like, to give a slightly tangy flavour. Serve warm.

Mayonnaise

MAKES 150ML/¼ PINT/⅔ CUP

1 egg yolk, at room temperature

15ml/1 tbsp lemon juice or white wine vinegar

5ml/1 tsp Dijon mustard

150ml/¼ pint/⅔ cup olive oil

1 Put the egg yolk in a bowl with the lemon juice or vinegar, mustard and a little salt. Whisk until combined.

2 Gradually add the oil in a very thin trickle, whisking continuously until the sauce is thickened and smooth.

3 Check the seasoning, adding a few drops of lemon juice or vinegar if the mayonnaise is too bland. If the sauce is too thick, stir in a few drops of warm water. Cover with clear film (plastic wrap) and store in the refrigerator for up to 2 days.

Flavoured Oils

Home-made flavoured oils are very economical, and you can have complete control over the ingredients you choose. Once made, the oil should be left in a cool place for up to a week to allow the flavours to infuse. Then the oil should be strained before storing. The aromatic ingredients should not be stored long term in the oil, because of the risk of harmful moulds developing.

Basil Oil Blend a large handful of basil leaves with 200ml/7fl oz/scant 1 cup olive oil in a food processor. Leave overnight, then strain through a muslin- (cheesecloth-) lined sieve into a clean bowl. Store in the refrigerator.

Garlic and Rosemary Oil Put a handful of fresh chillies into 120ml/4fl oz/½ cup olive oil in a small pan. Heat gently until bubbling, then pour into a heatproof bowl, cover and leave in a cool place overnight. Strain the oil into a clean bottle and top up with more oil. You can add some extra chillies to the oil for decorative purposes.

Melon Pick-me-up

Spicy fresh root ginger is delicious with melon and pear in this reviving and invigorating concoction. Charentais or Galia melon can be used instead of the cantaloupe melon. To enjoy fresh root ginger at its best, buy it in small quantities and keep in a cool, dry place for up to a week. As it ages, the root will dry out and become hard.

SERVES ONE

1 Quarter the cantaloupe melon, remove the seeds, and carefully slice the flesh away from the skin, reserving any juice. Quarter the pears.

2 Using a juice extractor, juice the melon flesh and juice, quartered pears and the fresh root ginger. Pour the juice into a tall glass and serve immediately.

½ cantaloupe melon

2 pears

2.5cm/1in piece of fresh root ginger

Apple Shiner

This fusion of apple, honeydew melon, red grapes and lemon provides a reviving burst of energy and a feel-good sensation. Serve as a drink or pour over granola for a quick and healthy breakfast.

SERVES ONE

1 eating apple

½ honeydew melon

90g/3½oz red grapes

15ml/1 tbsp lemon juice

1 Quarter the apple and remove the core. Cut the melon into quarters, remove the seeds and the skin.

2 Using a juice extractor, juice the apple, melon and grapes. Alternatively, process the fruit in a food processor or blender for 2–3 minutes, until smooth.

3 Pour the juice into a long, tall glass, stir in the lemon juice and serve immediately.

Citrus Sparkle

Zesty citrus fruits are packed with vitamin C, which is necessary for a healthy immune system. Pink grapefruit have a sweeter flavour than the yellow varieties – in fact, the pinker they are, the sweeter they are likely to be. For a lighter drink to serve two, divide the juice between two glasses and top up with sparkling mineral water and ice cubes.

SERVES ONE

1 Cut the pink grapefruit and orange in half and squeeze out the juice using a citrus fruit squeezer.

2 Pour the juice into a glass, stir in 15ml/1 tbsp lemon juice, add the remaining lemon juice if required and serve immediately.

1 pink grapefruit

1 orange

30ml/2 tbsp lemon juice

Mango Zinger

Aromatic tropical fruits make a drink that is bursting with flavour and energy. Enjoy a glass first thing in the morning to kick-start your day.

SERVES ONE

½ pineapple, peeled

1 small mango, peeled and stoned (pitted)

½ papaya, seeded and peeled

1 Remove any 'eyes' left in the pineapple, then cut all the fruit into fairly coarse chunks.

2 Using a juice extractor, juice the fruit. Alternatively, use a food processor or blender and process for about 2–3 minutes until smooth. Pour into a glass and serve immediately.

Strawberry and Banana Smoothie

The blend of perfectly ripe bananas and strawberries creates a drink that is both fruity and creamy, with a luscious texture. Mango can be used instead of strawberries for a tropical drink. This is a great way to get children to enjoy fruit.

SERVES FOUR

200g/7oz/1¾ cups strawberries, hulled, plus extra, sliced, to decorate

2 ripe bananas

300ml/½ pint/1¼ cups skimmed milk

10 ice cubes

1 Peel the bananas and chop them into fairly large chunks. Put the bananas and strawberries in a food processor or blender. Process to a thick, coarse purée, scraping down the sides of the goblet as necessary.

2 Add the skimmed milk and ice cubes, crushing the ice first unless you have a heavy-duty processor. Process until smooth and thick. Pour into tall glasses and top with strawberry slices. Serve immediately.

Raspberry and Orange Smoothie

Sharp-sweet raspberries and zesty oranges taste fabulous combined with the light creaminess of yogurt. This smoothie takes just minutes to prepare, making it perfect for a quick weekday breakfast.

SERVES TWO TO THREE

1 Place the raspberries and yogurt in a food processor or blender and process for about 1 minute, until smooth and creamy.

2 Add the orange juice to the raspberry and yogurt mixture and process for about 30 seconds, until thoroughly combined. Pour into tall glasses and serve immediately.

250g/9oz/1½ cups fresh raspberries, chilled

200ml/7fl oz/scant 1 cup natural (plain) yogurt, chilled

300ml/½ pint/1¼ cups freshly squeezed orange juice, chilled

COOK'S TIP For a super-chilled version, use frozen raspberries instead of fresh. You may need to blend the raspberries and yogurt slightly longer for a really smooth result.

Vanilla and Chocolate Latte

This luxurious vanilla and chocolate version of the classic coffee drink can be served at any time of the day. For an extra treat try topping the coffee with whipped cream and stir with a cinnamon stick to flavour the drink.

SERVES TWO

1 Pour the milk into a small pan and bring to the boil, then remove from the heat. Mix the coffee with 500ml/16fl oz/2 cups of the boiled milk in a large heatproof jug or pitcher.

2 Return the remaining boiled milk in the pan to the heat and add the 45ml/3 tbsp vanilla sugar. Stir constantly until dissolved. Bring to the boil, then reduce the heat. Add the dark chocolate and continue to heat, stirring constantly until all the chocolate has melted and the mixture is smooth and glossy.

3 Pour the chocolate milk into the jug of coffee and whisk thoroughly.

700ml/24fl oz/scant 3 cups milk

250ml/8fl oz/1 cup espresso or very strong coffee

45ml/3 tbsp vanilla sugar, plus extra to taste

115g/4oz dark (bittersweet) chocolate, grated

Frothy Hot Chocolate

Real hot chocolate doesn't come as a powder in a packet – it is made with the best chocolate you can afford, whisked in hot milk until really frothy. This recipe uses dark (bittersweet) chocolate, but for a special treat you could use Mexican chocolate, which is flavoured with almonds, cinnamon and vanilla, and sweetened with sugar.

SERVES FOUR

1 Pour the milk into a pan. Split the vanilla pod lengthways using a sharp knife to reveal the seeds, and add it to the milk.

2 Add the chocolate. The amount to use depends on personal taste – start with a smaller amount if you are unsure of the flavour and taste at the beginning of step 3.

3 Heat the chocolate milk gently, stirring until all the chocolate has melted and the mixture is smooth, then whisk with a wire whisk until the mixture boils. .

4 Remove the vanilla pod from the pan and divide the drink among four mugs or heatproof glasses. Serve immediately.

1 litre/1¾ pints/4 cups milk

50–115g/ 2–4oz dark (bittersweet) chocolate, grated

1 vanilla pod (bean)

Avocado Soup with Coriander

This delicious soup has a fresh, delicate flavour and a wonderful colour. For added zest, add a generous squeeze of lime juice or spoon 15ml/1 tbsp pesto into the soup just before serving. It's imortant to use very ripe avocados for this soup – they should feel soft when gently pressed.

SERVES FOUR

1 Cut the avocados in half, remove the peel and lift out the stones (pits). Chop the flesh coarsely and place it in a food processor with 45–60ml/ 3–4 tbsp of the sour cream. Process until smooth.

2 Heat the chicken stock in a pan. When it is hot, but still below simmering point, stir in the rest of the cream with salt to taste.

3 Gradually stir the avocado mixture into the hot stock. Heat gently but do not let the mixture approach boiling point. Serve in warmed bowls topped with chopped coriander and black pepper.

2 large ripe avocados

300ml/½ pint/1¼ cups sour cream

1 litre/1¾ pints/ 4 cups well-flavoured chicken stock

a few sprigs fresh coriander (cilantro), chopped

Leek and Potato Soup

This classic, chilled summer soup of leeks and potatoes was first created in the 1920s by Louis Diat, chef at the New York Ritz-Carlton. The soup can be enriched with swirls of cream and garnished with chives.

SERVES FOUR TO SIX

1 Melt the unsalted butter in a heavy pan and cook the leeks, covered, for 15–20 minutes, until they are soft but not browned.

2 Add the potato chunks and cook over a low heat, uncovered, for a few minutes.

3 Stir in the stock or water and milk, with salt and pepper to taste. Bring to the boil, then reduce the heat and partly cover the pan. Simmer for 15 minutes, or until the potatoes are soft.

4 Cool, then process the soup until smooth in a blender or food processor. Sieve the soup into a bowl. Taste and adjust the seasoning and add a little iced water if the consistency of the soup seems too thick.

5 Chill the soup for at least 4 hours or until very cold. Taste the chilled soup for seasoning again before serving. Pour the soup into bowls and serve.

50g/2oz/¼ cup unsalted (sweet) butter

600g/1lb 5oz leeks, white parts only, thinly sliced

250g/9oz floury potatoes (such as King Edward or Maris Piper), peeled and cut into chunks

1.5 litres/2½ pints/6½ cups half and half light chicken stock or water and milk

Butter Bean, Sun-dried Tomato and Pesto Soup

This soup is so quick and easy to make: the key is to use a good-quality home-made or bought fresh stock for the best result. Using plenty of pesto and sun-dried tomato purée gives it a rich, minestrone-like flavour. When serving, add a swirl of tomato purée to each bowl.

SERVES FOUR

1 Put the stock in a pan with the butter beans and bring just to the boil. Reduce the heat and stir in the tomato purée and pesto. Cook gently for 5 minutes.

2 Transfer six ladlefuls of the soup to a blender or food processor, scooping up plenty of the beans. Process until smooth, then return the purée back to the pan.

3 Heat gently, stirring frequently, for 5 minutes, then season if necessary. Ladle into four warmed soup bowls and serve with warm crusty bread or breadsticks.

900ml/1½ pints/ 3¾ cups chicken stock

2 x 400g/14oz cans butter (lima) beans, drained

60ml/4 tbsp sun-dried tomato purée (paste)

75ml/5 tbsp pesto

Stilton and Watercress Soup

A good creamy Stilton and plenty of peppery watercress bring maximum flavour to this rich, smooth soup, which is superlative in small portions. Rocket (arugula) can be used as an alternative to watercress – both leaves are an excellent source of iron.

SERVES FOUR TO SIX

1 Pour the stock into a pan and bring almost to the boil. Remove and discard any very large stalks from the watercress. Add the watercress to the pan and simmer gently for 2–3 minutes, until tender.

2 Crumble the cheese into the pan and simmer for 1 minute more, until the cheese has started to melt.

3 Process the soup in a blender or food processor, in batches if necessary, until very smooth. Return the soup to the pan.

4 Stir in the cream and check the seasoning. The soup will probably not need any extra salt, as the blue cheese is quite salty. Heat the soup gently, without boiling, then ladle it into warm bowls and sprinkle a few finely chopped watercress leaves.

600ml/1 pint/ 2½ cups chicken or vegetable stock

225g/8oz watercress, plus extra finely chopped, to serve

150g/5oz Stilton or other blue cheese

150ml/¼ pint/⅔ cup single (light) cream

Mushroom Caviar

The name caviar refers to the dark colour and texture of the chopped mushrooms. Serve this mushroom mixture in individual serving dishes with toasted rye bread rubbed with cut garlic cloves, to accompany. Chopped hard-boiled egg, spring onion and parsley, the traditional garnishes for caviar, can be added as a garnish.

SERVES FOUR

1 Heat the oil in a large pan, add the mushrooms, shallots and garlic, and cook, stirring occasionally, until browned. Season with salt, then continue cooking until the mushrooms give up their liquor.

2 Continue cooking, stirring frequently, until the liquor has evaporated and the mushrooms are brown and dry.

3 Put the mixture in a food processor or blender and process briefly until a chunky paste is formed. Spoon the mushroom caviar into dishes and serve.

45ml/3 tbsp olive or vegetable oil

450g/1lb mushrooms, coarsely chopped

5–10 shallots, chopped

4 garlic cloves, chopped

EXTRAS *For wild mushroom caviar, soak 15g/½oz dried porcini in 120ml/ 4fl oz/½ cup water for 30 minutes. Add the porcini and their soaking liquid to the browned mushrooms in step 2. Continue as in the recipe.*

Walnut and Goat's Cheese Toasts

The combination of toasted walnuts and melting goat's cheese is lovely in this simple appetizer, served with a pile of salad leaves. Toasting the walnuts helps to enhance their flavour. Walnut bread is readily available in most large supermarkets and makes an interesting alternative to ordinary crusty bread, although this can be used if walnut bread is unavailable.

SERVES FOUR

COOK'S TIP *Use walnut bread slices from a slender loaf, so that the portions are not too wide. If you can buy only a large loaf, cut the slices in half to make chunky pieces.*

1 Preheat the grill (broiler). Lightly toast the walnut pieces, then remove and set aside. Put the walnut bread on a foil-lined grill rack and toast on one side. Turn the slices over and drizzle each with 15ml/1 tbsp of the French dressing.

2 Cut the goat's cheese into twelve slices and place three on each piece of bread. Grill (broil) for about 3 minutes, until the cheese is golden brown.

3 Transfer the toasts to serving plates, sprinkle with the toasted walnuts and drizzle with the remaining French dressing.

50g/2oz/½ cup walnut pieces

4 thick slices walnut bread

120ml/4fl oz/½ cup French dressing

200g/7oz semi-soft goat's cheese

Chopped Egg and Onions

This dish is one of the oldest dishes in Jewish culinary history. It is delicious served sprinkled with chopped parsley and onion rings on crackers, piled on toast, or used as a sandwich or bagel filling.

SERVES FOUR TO SIX

1 Put the eggs in a large pan and cover with cold water. Bring the water to the boil and when it boils, reduce the heat and simmer over a low heat for 10 minutes.

2 Hold the boiled eggs under cold running water (if too hot to handle, place the eggs in a strainer and hold under the running water). When cool, shell the eggs, and chop coarsely.

3 Place the chopped eggs in a large bowl, add the onions, season generously with salt and black pepper and mix well. Add enough mayonnaise to bind the mixture together. Stir in the mustard, if using, and chill before serving.

8–10 eggs

6–8 spring onions (scallions) and/or 1 yellow or white onion, very finely chopped, plus extra to garnish

60–90ml/4–6 tbsp mayonnaise

wholegrain mustard, to taste

Feta Cheese with Green Olives

Mild white cheeses spiked with seasonings, such as this one that is flavoured with piquant green olives, are delicious served with drinks and little crackers or toast. It is also very good served for brunch – spread generously on chunks of crusty bread or bagels.

SERVES FOUR

175–200g/ 6–7oz soft white (farmer's) cheese

65g/2½ oz feta cheese

20–30 pitted green olives, some chopped, the rest halved

2–3 sprigs fresh thyme, plus extra to garnish

1 Place the soft white cheese in a mixing bowl and stir with the back of a spoon or a fork until soft and smooth.

2 Add the crumbled feta cheese and stir the two cheeses together until they are thoroughly combined.

3 Add the chopped, halved and quartered olives and the pinches of fresh thyme to the cheese mixture and mix thoroughly.

4 Spoon the mixture into a bowl, sprinkle with thyme and serve. It will keep in the fridge for up to 2 days.

Poached Fish in Spicy Tomato Sauce

A selection of white fish fillets can be used in this dish – cod, haddock, hake or halibut are all suitable. Serve the fish with flat breads, such as pitta, and a spicy tomato relish. It is also good with couscous or rice and a green salad with a refreshing lemon juice dressing.

SERVES EIGHT

1 Heat the tomato sauce with the harissa and coriander in a large pan. Add seasoning and bring to the boil.

2 Remove the pan from the heat and add the fish to the hot sauce. Return to the heat and bring the sauce to the boil again. Reduce the heat and simmer very gently for about 5 minutes, or until the fish is tender. (Test with a fork: if the flesh flakes easily, then it is cooked.)

3 Taste the sauce and adjust the seasoning, adding more harissa if necessary. Serve hot or warm.

600ml/1 pint/2½ cups fresh tomato sauce

2.5–5ml/½–1 tsp harissa

60ml/4 tbsp chopped fresh coriander (cilantro) leaves

1.5kg/3¼lb mixed white fish fillets, cut into chunks

COOK'S TIP *Harissa is a chilli paste spiced with cumin, garlic and coriander. It is fiery and should be used with care. Start by adding a small amount and then add more after tasting the sauce.*

Filo-wrapped Fish

Select a chunky variety of tomato sauce for this simple but delicious recipe. The choice of fish can be varied according to what is in season and what is freshest on the day of purchase. When working with filo pastry, keep it covered with clear film (plastic wrap) or a damp dishtowel, as once it's exposed to air it dries out quickly and is difficult to handle.

SERVES THREE TO FOUR

about 130g/ 4½oz filo pastry (6–8 large sheets)

about 30ml/ 2 tbsp olive oil, for brushing

450g/1lb salmon or cod steaks or fillets

550ml/18fl oz/ 2½ cups fresh tomato sauce

1 Preheat the oven to 200°C/400°F/Gas 6. Take a sheet of filo pastry, brush with a little olive oil and cover with a second sheet of pastry. Place a piece of fish on top of the pastry, towards the bottom edge, then top with 1–2 spoonfuls of the tomato sauce, spreading it in an even layer.

2 Roll the fish in the pastry, taking care to enclose the filling completely. Brush with a little olive oil. Arrange on a baking sheet and repeat with the remaining fish and pastry. You should have about half the sauce remaining, to serve with the fish.

3 Bake for 10–15 minutes, or until golden. Meanwhile, reheat the remaining sauce. Serve the fish immediately with the sauce drizzled over.

Baked Salmon with Green Sauce

When buying whole salmon, there are several points to consider – the skin should be bright and shiny, the eyes should be bright and the tail should look fresh and moist. Baking the salmon in foil produces a moist result, rather like poaching, but with the ease of baking. Garnish the fish with thin slices of cucumber and dill to conceal any flesh that may look ragged after skinning, and serve with lemon wedges.

SERVES SIX TO EIGHT

2–3kg/4½–6¾ lb salmon, cleaned, head and tail left on

3–5 spring onions (scallions), thinly sliced

1 lemon, thinly sliced

600ml/1 pint/2½ cups watercress sauce or herb mayonnaise

1 cucumber, washed and very finely sliced, to garnish

sprigs of fresh dill, to garnish

1 Preheat the oven to 180°C/350°F/Gas 4. Rinse the salmon and lay it on a large piece of foil. Stuff the fish with the sliced spring onions and layer the lemon slices inside and around the fish, then sprinkle with plenty of salt and ground black pepper.

2 Loosely fold the foil around the fish and fold the edges over to seal. Bake for about 1 hour.

3 Remove the fish from the oven and leave to stand, still wrapped in the foil, for about 15 minutes, then unwrap the parcel and leave the fish to cool.

4 When the fish is cool, carefully lift it on to a large plate, retaining the lemon slices. Cover the fish tightly with clear film (plastic wrap) and chill for several hours.

5 Before serving, discard the lemon slices from around the fish. Using a blunt knife to lift up the edge of the skin, carefully peel the skin away from the flesh, avoiding tearing the flesh, and pull out any fins at the same time.

6 Chill the watercress sauce or herb mayonnaise before serving. Transfer the fish to a serving platter, garnish with the cucumber slices and dill and serve the sauce separately.

> **VARIATION**
> Instead of cooking a whole fish, prepare 6–8 salmon steaks. Place each fish steak on an individual square of foil, then top with a slice of onion and a slice of lemon and season generously with salt and ground black pepper. Loosely wrap the foil up around the fish, fold the edges to seal and place the parcels on a baking sheet. Bake the steaks for 10–15 minutes, or until the flesh is opaque. Serve the fish cold with the chilled watercress sauce or herb mayonnaise.

Haddock with Fennel Butter

Fresh fish tastes fabulous cooked in a simple herb butter. Here the liquorice flavour of fennel complements the haddock beautifully to make a simple dish ideal for a dinner party. If you buy small haddock fillets, fold them in half before baking. Serve tiny new potatoes and a herb salad with the fish to make a light, summery main course.

SERVES FOUR

1 Preheat the oven to 220°C/425°F/Gas 7. Season the fish on both sides with salt and pepper. Melt one-quarter of the butter in a frying pan, and cook the fish over a medium heat briefly on both sides.

2 Transfer the fish to a shallow ovenproof dish. Cut four wafer-thin slices from the lemon and squeeze the juice from the remainder over the fish. Place the lemon slices on top and then bake for 15–20 minutes, or until the fish is cooked.

3 Meanwhile, melt the remaining butter in the frying pan and add the fennel and a little seasoning.

4 Transfer the fish to plates and pour the cooking juices into the herb butter. Heat gently for a few seconds, then pour over the fish and serve.

675g/1½lb haddock fillet, skinned and cut into 4 portions

50g/2oz/¼ cup butter

1 lemon

45ml/3 tbsp coarsely chopped fennel

Crab and Cucumber Wraps

This dish is a modern twist on the ever-popular Chinese classic, crispy Peking duck with pancakes. In this quick and easy version, crisp, refreshing cucumber and full-flavoured dressed crab are delicious with spicy-sweet hoisin sauce in warm tortilla wraps. Serve the wraps as an appetizer for four people, or as a main course for two.

SERVES TWO

1 Cut the cucumber into small even-sized batons. Scoop the dressed crab into a small mixing bowl, add a little freshly ground black pepper and mix lightly with a fork to combine.

2 Heat the tortillas gently, one at a time, in a heavy frying pan until they begin to colour on each side.

3 Spread a tortilla with 30ml/2 tbsp hoisin sauce, then sprinkle with one-quarter of the cucumber. Arrange one-quarter of the seasoned crab meat down the centre of each tortilla and roll up. Repeat with the remaining ingredients. Serve immediately.

½ cucumber

1 medium dressed crab

4 small wheat tortillas

120ml/8 tbsp hoisin sauce

Scallops with Fennel and Bacon

This dish is a delicious combination of succulent scallops and crispy bacon, served on a bed of tender fennel and melting mascarpone. If you can't get large scallops (known as king scallops), buy the smaller queen scallops and serve a dozen per person. If you buy scallops in the shell, wash and keep the shells to serve a range of fish dishes in.

SERVES TWO

1 Trim, halve and slice the fennel, reserving and chopping any feathery tops. Blanch the slices in boiling water for about 3 minutes, until softened, then drain.

2 Preheat the grill (broiler) to moderate. Place the fennel in a shallow flameproof dish and season with salt and pepper. Dot with the mascarpone and grill (broil) for about 5 minutes, until the cheese has melted and the fennel is lightly browned.

3 Meanwhile, pat the scallops dry on kitchen paper and season lightly. Cook the bacon in a large, heavy frying pan, until crisp and golden, turning once. Drain and keep warm. Fry the scallops in the bacon fat for 1–2 minutes on each side, until cooked through.

4 Transfer the fennel to serving plates and crumble or snip the bacon over the top. Pile the scallops on the bacon and sprinkle with reserved fennel tops.

2 small fennel bulbs

130g/4½oz/ generous ½ cup mascarpone cheese

8 large scallops, shelled

75g/3oz thin smoked streaky (fatty) bacon rashers (strips)

Prawn and New Potato Stew

New potatoes with plenty of flavour, such as Jersey Royals, Maris Piper or Nicola, are essential for this effortless stew. Use a good quality jar of tomato and chilli sauce; there are now plenty available in the supermarkets. For a really easy supper dish, serve with warm, crusty bread to mop up the delicious sauce, and a mixed green salad.

SERVES FOUR

675g/1½lb small new potatoes, scrubbed

15g/½oz/½ cup fresh coriander (cilantro)

350g/12oz jar tomato and chilli sauce

300g/11oz cooked peeled prawns (shrimp)

1 Cook the potatoes in lightly salted, boiling water for 15 minutes, until tender. Drain and return to the pan.

2 Finely chop half the coriander and add to the pan with the tomato and chilli sauce and 90ml/6 tbsp water. Bring to the boil, reduce the heat, cover and simmer gently for 5 minutes.

3 Stir in the prawns and heat briefly until they are warmed through. Do not overheat the prawns or they will quickly shrivel, becoming tough and tasteless. Spoon into shallow bowls and serve sprinkled with the remaining coriander, torn into pieces.

FISH AND SHELLFISH

Beef Patties with Onions and Peppers

This is a firm family favourite. It is easy to make and delicious, and it can be varied by adding other vegetables, such as sliced red peppers, broccoli or mushrooms. These patties are very versatile and can be served in a variety of ways – with chunky home-made chips (fries), with crusty bread, or with rice and a ready-made tomato sauce.

SERVES FOUR

1 Place the minced beef, chopped onion and 15ml/ 1 tbsp oil in a bowl and mix well. Season well and form into four large or eight small patties.

2 Heat the remaining oil in a large non-stick pan, then add the patties and cook on both sides until browned. Sprinkle over 15ml/1 tbsp water and add seasoning.

3 Cover the patties with the sliced onions and peppers. Sprinkle in another 15ml/1 tbsp water and a little seasoning, then cover the pan. Reduce the heat to very low and braise for 20–30 minutes.

4 When the vegetables are soft and the onions are golden brown, remove from the heat and serve.

500g/1¼lb lean minced (ground) beef

4 onions, 1 finely chopped and 3 sliced

30ml/2 tbsp olive oil

2–3 green (bell) peppers, seeded and sliced lengthways into strips

Steak with Warm Tomato Salsa

A refreshing, tangy salsa of tomatoes, spring onions and balsamic vinegar makes a colourful topping for chunky, pan-fried steaks. Choose rump, sirloin or fillet – whichever is your favourite – and if you do not have a non-stick pan, grill the steak instead for the same length of time. Serve with potato wedges and a mixed leaf salad.

SERVES TWO

1 Trim any excess fat from the steaks, then season on both sides with salt and pepper.

2 Heat a non-stick frying pan and cook the steaks for about 3 minutes on each side for medium rare. Cook for a little longer if you like your steak well cooked. Transfer the steaks to plates and keep warm.

3 Meanwhile, put the tomatoes in a heatproof bowl, cover with boiling water and leave for 1–2 minutes, until the skins start to split. Drain and peel the tomatoes, then halve them and scoop out the seeds. Dice the tomato flesh. Thinly slice the spring onions.

4 Add the vegetables, balsamic vinegar, 30ml/2 tbsp water and a little seasoning to the cooking juices in the pan and stir briefly until warm, scraping up any meat residue. Spoon the salsa over the steaks to serve.

2 steaks, about 2cm/³⁄₄in thick

4 large plum tomatoes

2 spring onions (scallions)

30ml/2 tbsp balsamic vinegar

Fruity Lamb

This dish is full of contrasting flavours that create a rich, spicy and fruity main course. For best results, use lamb that still retains some fat, as this will help keep the meat moist and succulent during roasting. Serve the lamb with couscous or mixed white and wild rice, sprinkled with chopped coriander.

SERVES FOUR

1 Preheat the oven to 200°C/400°F/Gas 6. Season the lamb with salt and pepper. Heat a frying pan, preferably non-stick, and cook the lamb on all sides until beginning to brown. Transfer to a roasting pan, reserving any fat in the frying pan.

2 Peel the onions and cut each into six wedges. Toss with the lamb and roast for about 30-40 minutes, until the lamb is cooked through and the onions are deep golden brown.

3 Tip the lamb and onions back into the frying pan. Mix the harissa with 250ml/8fl oz/1 cup boiling water and add to the roasting pan. Scrape up any residue in the pan and pour the mixture over the lamb and onions.

4 Stir in the prunes and heat until just simmering. Cover and simmer for 5 minutes, then serve.

675g/1½lb lamb fillet or shoulder steaks, cut into chunky pieces

5 small onions

7.5ml/1½ tsp harissa

115g/4oz ready-to-eat pitted prunes, halved

Lamb Steaks with Redcurrant Glaze

This simple dish is absolutely delicious and is an excellent, quick recipe for cooking on the barbecue. The tangy flavour of redcurrants is a traditional accompaniment to lamb. It is good served with new potatoes and fresh garden peas tossed in butter.

SERVES FOUR

1 Reserve the tips of the rosemary and finely chop the remaining leaves. Rub the chopped rosemary, salt and pepper all over the lamb. Light the barbecue or preheat the grill (broiler).

2 Heat the redcurrant jelly gently in a small pan with 30ml/2 tbsp water and a little seasoning. Add the vinegar.

3 Place the lamb steaks on the barbecue or a foil-lined grill (broiler) rack and brush with a little of the redcurrant glaze. Cook for about 5 minutes on each side, until deep golden, brushing frequently with more redcurrant glaze. Tip any juices from the foil into the remaining glaze and heat through gently. Pour over the lamb and serve.

4 large fresh rosemary sprigs

4 lamb leg steaks

75ml/5 tbsp redcurrant jelly

30ml/2 tbsp raspberry or red wine vinegar

Paprika Pork

This chunky, goulash-style dish is rich with peppers and paprika. Grilling the peppers before adding them to the meat really brings out their sweet, vibrant flavour. Rice or buttered boiled potatoes go particularly well with the rich pork.

SERVES FOUR

2 red, 1 yellow and 1 green (bell) pepper, seeded

500g/1¼lb lean pork fillet (tenderloin)

45ml/3 tbsp paprika

300g/11oz jar or tub of tomato sauce with herbs or garlic

1 Preheat the grill (broiler). Cut the peppers into thick strips and sprinkle in a single layer on a foil-lined grill rack. Cook under the grill for 20–25 minutes, until the edges of the strips are lightly charred.

2 Meanwhile, cut the pork into chunks. Season with salt and pepper and cook in a non-stick frying pan for about 5 minutes, until beginning to brown.

3 Transfer the meat to a heavy pan and add the paprika, tomato sauce, 300ml/½ pint/1¼ cups water and a little seasoning. Bring to the boil, reduce the heat, cover and simmer gently for 30 minutes.

4 Add the grilled (broiled) peppers and cook for a further 10–15 minutes, until the meat is tender. Taste for seasoning and serve immediately.

Pork Kebabs

The word kebab comes from Arabic and means on a skewer. Use pork fillet (tenderloin) for these kebabs because it is lean and tender, and cooks quickly. The kebabs are good served with rice, or stuffed into warmed pitta bread with some shredded lettuce leaves.

SERVES FOUR

1 Cut the pork into 2.5cm/1in cubes and place in a bowl with the barbecue sauce and set aside for 10–15 minutes. Cut the spring onions into 2.5cm/1in long sticks. Soak eight wooden or bamboo skewers in water for 10 minutes.

2 Preheat the grill (broiler) to high, and oil a wire rack. Thread about four pieces of pork and three spring onion pieces on to each of the soaked skewers.

3 Grill (broil) the pork until tender, cooked through and slightly charred, turning over half way through cooking and brushing with the barbecue sauce.

4 Arrange the skewers on a platter. Cut the lemon into wedges and squeeze a little lemon juice over each skewer. Serve with the remaining lemon wedges.

500g/1¼lb lean pork fillet (tenderloin)

8 large, thick spring onions (scallions), trimmed

120ml/4fl oz/ ½ cup barbecue sauce

1 lemon

Chicken Escalopes with Lemon Slices and Ham

Chicken escalopes are flattened chicken breast fillets – which cook quicker than normal breast portions and absorb flavours more readily. This light summery dish can be assembled in advance, so is good for entertaining.

SERVES FOUR

1 Preheat the oven to 180°C/350°F/Gas 4. Beat the butter with plenty of freshly ground black pepper and set aside. Place the chicken portions on a large sheet of clear film (plastic wrap), spacing them well apart. Cover with a second sheet, then beat with a rolling pin until the portions are half their original thickness.

2 Transfer the chicken to a large, shallow ovenproof dish and crumple a slice of ham on top of each. Cut eight thin slices from the lemon and place two on each slice of ham and dot with the pepper butter.

3 Bake for 20–30 minutes, until the chicken is cooked. Serve with any juices from the dish spooned on top.

40g/1½ oz/ 3 tbsp butter, softened

4 skinless chicken breast fillets

4 slices Serrano ham

1 lemon

Roast Chicken with Chilli and Lime Stuffing

Whether you are entertaining guests or cooking a family meal, a roast chicken is a sure winner every time. This version has stuffing under the chicken skin, which helps to produce a wonderfully flavoured, succulent result.

SERVES FIVE TO SIX

1 Preheat the oven to 200°C/400°F/Gas 6. Using your fingers, separate the skin from the meat across the chicken breast and over the tops of the legs, running your fingers underneath, taking care not to tear the skin.

2 Beat the lime zest and chilli into the cream cheese, adding salt and black pepper to taste. Pack the cream cheese stuffing under the skin until fairly evenly distributed. Push the skin back into place, then smooth your hands over it to spread the stuffing evenly.

3 Put the chicken in a roasting pan, squeeze the juice from the lime over the top and sprinkle with salt.

4 Roast for 1½ hours, or until the juices run clear when the thickest part of the thigh is pierced with a skewer. If necessary, cover the chicken with foil towards the end of cooking if the top starts to become too browned.

5 Allow the chicken to rest for at least 20 minutes then carve, arranging the slices on a warmed serving platter. Spoon the pan juices over and serve.

1.8kg/4lb chicken

grated zest and juice of 1 lime

115g/4oz/½ cup cream cheese with herbs and garlic

1 mild fresh red chilli, seeded and finely chopped

Soy-marinated Chicken

Two simple flavours, soy sauce and orange, combine to make this mouthwatering dish. Serving the chicken on a bed of asparagus turns the dish into a special treat. Wilted spinach or shredded greens work well as an everyday alternative. Boiled egg noodles or steamed white rice make a good accompaniment.

4 skinless, chicken breast fillets

1 large orange

30ml/2 tbsp soy sauce

400g/14oz medium asparagus spears

SERVES FOUR

1 Slash each chicken portion diagonally and place them in a single layer in a shallow, ovenproof dish. Halve the orange, squeeze the juice from one half and mix it with the soy sauce. Pour this over the chicken. Cut the remaining orange into wedges and place on top. Cover and leave to marinate for 4–6 hours.

2 Preheat the oven to 180°C/350°F/Gas 4. Turn the chicken over and bake, uncovered, for 12 minutes. Turn the chicken over again and bake for a further 12–15 minutes, or until cooked through.

3 Meanwhile, cut off any tough ends from the asparagus and place in a frying pan. Pour in enough boiling water just to cover and cook gently for 3–4 minutes, until just tender. Drain and arrange on warmed plates, then top with the chicken and orange wedges. Spoon over the cooking juices, season with pepper and serve.

Duck with Plum Sauce

Sharp plums cut the rich flavour of duck wonderfully well in this updated version of a traditional English dish. Duck is considered to be a fatty meat but modern breeding methods have made them leaner. For an easy dinner-party main course, serve the duck with creamy mashed potatoes, celeriac and steamed broccoli.

SERVES FOUR

4 duck quarters

1 large red onion, finely chopped

500g/1¼lb ripe plums, stoned (pitted) and quartered

30ml/2 tbsp redcurrant jelly

1 Prick the duck skin all over with a fork to release the fat during cooking and help give a crisp result, then place the portions in a heavy frying pan, skin side down.

2 Cook the duck pieces for 10 minutes on each side, or until golden brown and cooked right through. Remove the duck from the frying pan using a slotted spoon and keep warm.

3 Pour away all but 30ml/2 tbsp of the duck fat, then stir-fry the onion for 5 minutes, or until golden. Add the plums and cook for 5 minutes, stirring frequently. Add the jelly and mix well.

4 Replace the duck portions and cook for a further 5 minutes to heat through. Season before serving.

COOK'S TIP *It is important that the plums used in this dish are very ripe, otherwise the mixture will be too dry and the sauce will taste too sharp.*

Baby Squash Stuffed with Cheese and Rice

It is worth making the most of baby squash while they are in season. Use any varieties you can find and do not worry too much about choosing vegetables of uniform size, as an assortment of different types and sizes looks attractive. Serve with warm sun-dried tomato bread and a ready-made spicy tomato sauce for a hearty autumn supper.

SERVES FOUR

1 Preheat the oven to 190°C/375°F/Gas 5. Pierce the squash in several places with the tip of a knife. Bake for 30 minutes, until tender. Leave to cool.

2 Meanwhile, cook the rice in salted, boiling water for 12 minutes, until tender, then drain. Slice a lid off the top of each squash and scoop out and discard the seeds. Scoop out and chop the flesh.

3 Heat the oil in a frying pan and cook the chopped squash for 5 minutes. Reserving 60ml/4 tbsp of the cheese, mix the rest with the rice and a little salt.

4 Pile the mixture into the squash shells and place in an ovenproof dish. Sprinkle with the remaining cheese and bake for 20 minutes.

4 small squash, each about 350g/12oz

200g/7oz/1 cup mixed wild and basmati rice

60ml/4 tbsp chilli and garlic oil

150g/5oz/ 1¼ cups grated Gruyère cheese

Roasted Peppers with Halloumi and Pine Nuts

Halloumi cheese has a firm texture and salty flavour that contrasts well with the succulent sweet peppers. Halloumi is usually served cooked and lends itself well to barbecuing, frying or grilling (broiling), as it develops a crisp outside and soft interior. You need to eat it fairly soon after cooking, however, otherwise it becomes tough.

SERVES FOUR

1 Preheat the oven to 220°C/425°F/Gas 7. Halve the red peppers, leaving the stalks intact, and discard the seeds. Seed and coarsely chop the orange or yellow peppers. Place the red pepper halves on a baking sheet.

2 Fill the pepper halves with the chopped peppers. Drizzle with half the garlic or herb olive oil and bake for 25 minutes, until the edges of the peppers are beginning to char.

3 Dice the cheese and tuck in among the chopped peppers. Sprinkle with the pine nuts and drizzle with the remaining oil. Bake for a further 15 minutes, until well browned. Serve warm.

4 red and 2 orange or yellow (bell) peppers

60ml/4 tbsp garlic or herb olive oil

250g/9oz halloumi cheese

50g/2oz/½ cup pine nuts

Spicy Chickpea Samosas

Crisp pastry triangles filled with crushed chickpeas and coriander make an interesting alternative to the more familiar meat or vegetable fillings. The samosas look pretty garnished with fresh coriander leaves and finely sliced onion and are delicious served with a simple dip made from yogurt and chopped fresh mint leaves.

MAKES EIGHTEEN

1 Preheat the oven to 220°C/425°F/Gas 7. Process half the chickpeas to a paste in a food processor. Tip the paste into a bowl and add the whole chickpeas, the hara masala or coriander sauce, and a little salt. Mix well.

2 Lay a sheet of filo pastry on a work surface and cut into three strips. Brush the strips with a little of the oil. Place a dessertspoon of the filling at one end of a strip.

3 Turn one corner diagonally over the filling to meet the long edge. Continue folding the filling and the pastry along the length of the strip, keeping the triangular shape. Transfer to a baking sheet and repeat with the remaining filling and pastry.

4 Brush the pastries with any remaining oil and bake for 15 minutes, until the pastry is golden. Cool slightly before serving.

2 x 400g/14oz cans chickpeas, drained and rinsed

120ml/4fl oz/ ½ cup hara masala or coriander (cilantro) sauce

275g/10oz filo pastry

60ml/4 tbsp chilli and garlic oil

Tofu and Pepper Kebabs

A simple coating of ground, dry-roasted peanuts pressed on to cubed tofu provides plenty of additional flavour along with the peppers. If you use wooden skewers, soak them in cold water for 30 minutes before using to prevent them from scorching during cooking. The kebabs can also be cooked on a barbecue, if you prefer.

SERVES FOUR

1 Pat the tofu dry on kitchen paper and cut into small cubes. Grind the peanuts in a blender or food processor and transfer to a plate. Turn the tofu cubes in the ground nuts to coat.

2 Preheat the grill (broiler) to moderate. Halve and seed the peppers, and cut them into large chunks. Thread the pepper on to four large skewers alternating with the tofu cubes, and place on a foil-lined grill rack.

3 Grill (broil) the kebabs for 10–12 minutes, turning occasionally, until the peppers and peanuts are beginning to brown. Transfer the kebabs to plates and serve with the dipping sauce.

250g/9oz firm tofu

50g/2oz/½ cup dry-roasted peanuts

2 red and 2 green (bell) peppers

60ml/4 tbsp sweet chilli dipping sauce

Fettucine with Parmesan and Cream

Today's busy cooks will find cartons of long-life cream invaluable for this type of recipe. If you can't get fettucine, any long ribbon-like pasta can be used in this dish – try tagliatelle or slightly wider pappardelle instead.

SERVES FOUR

1 Melt the butter in a large pan. Add the cream and bring to the boil. Simmer for 5 minutes, stirring, then add the Parmesan cheese, with salt and black pepper to taste. Turn off the heat under the pan.

2 Bring a large pan of salted water to the boil. Add the pasta and quickly bring the water back to the boil, stirring occasionally. Cook the pasta for 2–3 minutes, following the instructions on the packet. Drain well.

3 Turn on the heat under the pan of cream to low, add the cooked pasta all at once and toss until it is thoroughly coated in the sauce. Taste for seasoning. Serve with extra grated Parmesan.

50g/2oz/¼ cup butter

200ml/7fl oz/ scant 1 cup double (heavy) cream

50g/2oz/²⁄₃ cup grated Parmesan cheese, plus extra to serve

350g/12oz fresh fettucine

Tagliatelle with Vegetable Ribbons

Narrow strips of courgette and carrot mingle with tagliatelle to resemble coloured pasta. Serve as a side dish, or sprinkle with freshly grated Parmesan cheese for a main course. The garlic-flavoured olive oil adds extra punch to this healthy dish.

SERVES FOUR

2 large courgettes (zucchini)

2 large carrots

250g/9oz fresh egg tagliatelle

60ml/4 tbsp garlic-flavoured olive oil

1 With a vegetable peeler, cut the courgettes and carrots into long thin ribbons. Bring a large pan of salted water to the boil, then add the courgette and carrot ribbons. Boil for 30 seconds, then drain and set aside.

2 Cook the tagliatelle according to the instructions on the packet. Drain and return to the pan.

3 Add the vegetable ribbons, garlic-flavoured oil and seasoning and toss over a medium to high heat until the pasta and vegetables are coated with oil. Serve.

Risotto with Borlotti Beans

Select a high-quality risotto in a subtle flavour as the base for this recipe. The savoury beans, heady rosemary and creamy mascarpone transforms a simple product into a feast. For an even more authentic risotto flavour, substitute half the water with white wine. Serve with salad of mixed leaves dressed with balsamic vinegar and plenty of freshly ground black pepper.

SERVES THREE TO FOUR

400g/14oz can borlotti beans

275g/10oz packet risotto rice

60ml/4 tbsp mascarpone cheese

5ml/1 tsp fresh rosemary, chopped

1 Drain the beans, rinse under cold water and drain again. Process about two-thirds of the beans to a fairly coarse purée in a food processor or blender. Set the remaining beans aside.

2 Make up the risotto according to the packet instructions, using the suggested quantity of stock or water.

3 Immediately the rice is cooked, stir in the bean purée. Add the reserved beans, with the mascarpone and rosemary, then season to taste.

4 Stir, then cover and leave to stand for about 5 minutes before serving so that the flavours are absorbed.

VARIATION *Fresh thyme or marjoram could be used for this risotto instead of rosemary. Experiment with plain or saffron risotto and add different herbs to make your own version.*

Bacon and Broad Bean Risotto

This moist risotto makes a satisfying, balanced meal, especially when served with a mixed green salad. Add some chopped fresh herbs and Parmesan shavings as a garnish, if you like.

SERVES FOUR

1 Place the pancetta in a non-stick or heavy pan and cook gently, stirring occasionally, for about 5 minutes, until the fat runs.

2 Add the risotto rice to the pan and cook for 1 minute, stirring constantly. Add a ladleful of the simmering stock and cook, still stirring, until the liquid is absorbed.

3 Continue adding the simmering stock, a ladleful at a time, until the rice is tender, and almost all the liquid has been absorbed. This will take 30–35 minutes.

4 Meanwhile, drain the broad beans and when cool enough to handle, slip them out of their skins. Stir into the risotto. Season to taste and serve.

175g/6oz smoked pancetta, diced

350g/12oz/ 1¾ cups risotto rice

1.5 litres/ 2½ pints/6¼ cups simmering herb stock

225g/8oz/ 2 cups frozen baby broad (fava) beans, cooked in boiling water for 3 minutes

Coconut and Lime Ice

The creamy taste and texture of this ice cream comes from the natural fat content of fresh coconut, as the mixture contains neither cream nor egg. The lime adds a delicious tangy flavour as well as pretty green specks to the refreshing finished ice. Decorate the top with toasted coconut shavings, see Cook's Tip.

SERVES FOUR TO SIX

115g/4oz/½ cup caster (superfine) sugar

2 limes

400ml/14fl oz can coconut milk

toasted coconut shavings, to decorate (optional)

1 Pour 150ml/¼ pint/⅔ cup water in a small pan. Tip in the sugar and bring to the boil, stirring constantly until the sugar has completely dissolved. Remove the pan from the heat and leave to cool, then chill well.

2 Grate the rind from the limes finely. Squeeze out their juice and add to the pan of cooled syrup with the rind. Add the coconut milk.

3 Pour the mixture into a freezerproof container and freeze for 5–6 hours, or until firm. Beat twice with a fork or electric whisk, or process in a food processor to break up the crystals. Scoop into dishes and decorate with toasted coconut shavings, if you like.

COOK'S TIP
For toasted coconut shavings, shave fresh coconut with a vegetable peeler, then toast under a grill (broiler) until the shavings curl, and are golden at the edges.

Blackberry Ice Cream

There could scarcely be fewer ingredients in this delicious, vibrant ice cream, which is simple to make and ideal as a prepare-ahead dessert. Serve the ice cream with buttery shortbread or almond biscuits, to provide a delicious contrast in taste and texture to the intensely tangy ice.

SERVES FOUR TO SIX

500g/1¼lb/5 cups blackberries, plus extra to decorate

75g/3oz/6 tbsp caster (superfine) sugar

300ml/½ pint/ 1¼ cups whipping cream

1 Put the blackberries into a pan, add 30ml/2 tbsp water and the sugar. Cover and simmer for 5 minutes, until just soft.

2 Tip the fruit into a sieve placed over a bowl and press it through the mesh, using a wooden spoon. Leave to cool, then chill.

3 Whip the cream until it is just thick but still soft enough to fall from a spoon, then mix it with the chilled fruit purée. Pour the mixture into a freezerproof container and freeze for 2 hours unti.

4 Mash the mixture with a fork or process it in a food processor to break up the ice crystals. Return it to the freezer for 4 hours more, mashing or processing the mixture again after 2 hours.

5 Scoop the ice cream into dishes and decorate with extra blackberries. Serve with crisp dessert biscuits.

White Chocolate and Brownie Torte

This delicious dessert is easy to make and guaranteed to appeal to just about everyone. If you can't buy good quality brownies, use a moist chocolate sponge or make your own. Put a few fresh summer berries around the edge or on the centre of the torte if you wish.

SERVES TEN

300g/11oz white chocolate, broken into pieces

600ml/ 1 pint/2½ cups double (heavy) cream

250g/9oz rich chocolate brownies

(unsweetened) cocoa powder, for dusting

1 Dampen the sides of a 20cm/8in springform tin or pan and line with a strip of greaseproof or waxed paper. Put the chocolate in a small pan. Add 150ml/¼ pint/⅔ cup of the cream and heat very gently until the chocolate has melted. Stir until smooth, then pour into a bowl and leave to cool.

2 Break the chocolate brownies into chunky pieces and sprinkle these over the base of the tin. Pack them down lightly to make a fairly dense base.

3 Whip the remaining cream until it forms peaks, then fold in the white chocolate mixture. Spoon into the tin to cover the layer of brownies, then tap the tin gently on the work surface to level the chocolate mixture. Cover and freeze overnight.

4 Transfer the torte to the refrigerator about 45 minutes before serving to soften slightly. Decorate with a light dusting of cocoa powder just before serving.

Summer Berries and Meringue Gâteau

This recipe takes only five minutes to prepare but looks and tastes as though a lot of preparation went into it. The trick is to use really good vanilla ice cream. For a dinner party, slice the gâteau and serve with raspberry coulis and whole strawberries.

SERVES SIX

1 Dampen a 900g/2lb loaf tin or pan and line it with clear film (plastic wrap). If using strawberries, chop them into small pieces. Put them in a bowl and add the other berries and icing sugar. Toss until the fruit is beginning to break up, but do not let it become mushy.

2 Put the ice cream in a bowl and break it up with a fork. Crumble the meringues into the bowl and add the soft fruit mixture.

3 Fold all the ingredients together until evenly combined and lightly marbled. Pack into the prepared tin and press down gently to level. Cover and freeze overnight. To serve, invert on to a plate and peel away the clear film. Serve in slices.

400g/14oz/3½ cups summer berries

30ml/2 tbsp icing (confectioners') sugar

750ml/1¼ pints/3 cups vanilla ice cream

6 meringue nests

Baked Caramel Custard

Many countries have their own version of this classic dessert. Known as crème caramel in France and flan in Spain, this chilled baked custard has a rich caramel flavour. By cooking the custard in a bain-marie or as here in a roasting pan with water, the mixture is cooked gently. It is delicious served with fresh strawberries and thick cream.

SERVES SIX TO EIGHT

1 Put 175g/6oz/generous ¾ cup of the sugar in a small heavy pan with just enough water to moisten the sugar. Bring to the boil over a high heat, swirling the pan until the sugar has dissolved completely. Boil for about 5 minutes, without stirring, until the syrup turns a rich, dark caramel colour.

2 Working quickly, pour the caramel into a 1 litre/1¼ pint/4 cup soufflé dish. Carefully swirl it to coat the base and sides with the hot caramel mixture. Set aside to cool.

250g/9oz/1¼ cups vanilla sugar

5 large (US extra large) eggs, plus 2 extra yolks

450ml/¾ pint/scant 2 cups double (heavy) cream

3 Preheat the oven to 160°C/325°F/Gas 3. In a bowl, whisk the eggs and egg yolks with the remaining sugar for 2–3 minutes, until smooth and creamy.

4 Heat the cream in a heavy pan until hot, but not boiling. Whisk the hot cream into the egg mixture and carefully strain the mixture into the caramel-lined dish. Cover tightly with foil.

5 Place the dish in a roasting pan and pour in just enough boiling water to come halfway up the side of the dish. Bake the custard for 40–45 minutes, until just set. To test whether the custard is set, insert a knife about 5cm/2in from the edge; if the blade comes out clean, the custard should be ready.

VARIATION *For a special occasion, make individual custards in ramekin dishes. Coat six to eight ramekins with the caramel and divide the custard mixture among them. Bake, in a roasting pan of water, for 25–30 minutes or until set. Thinly slice the strawberries and marinate them in a little sugar and dessert wine, such as Muscat.*

6 Remove the soufflé dish from the roasting pan and leave to cool for at least 30 minutes, then place in the refrigerator and chill overnight.

7 To turn out, carefully run a sharp knife around the edge of the dish to loosen the custard. Cover the dish with a serving plate and, holding them both together very tightly, invert the dish and plate, allowing the custard to drop down on to the plate.

8 Gently lift one edge of the dish, allowing the caramel to run down over the sides and on to the plate, then carefully lift off the dish to serve.

Grilled Peaches with Meringues

Ripe peaches take on a fabulous scented fruitiness when grilled with brown sugar, and mini meringues are the perfect accompaniment. Serve with crème fraîche flavoured with a little grated orange rind.

SERVES SIX

1 Preheat the oven to 140°C/275°F/Gas 1. Line two large baking sheets with baking parchment.

2 Whisk the egg whites until they form stiff peaks. Gradually whisk in the sugar and ground cinnamon until the mixture is stiff and glossy.

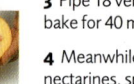

3 Pipe 18 very small meringues on to the trays and bake for 40 minutes. Leave in the oven to cool.

4 Meanwhile, halve and stone (pit) the peaches or nectarines, sprinkling each half with a little sugar as it is cut. Grill (broil) for 4–5 minutes, until just beginning to caramelize.

5 Arrange the grilled peaches on serving plates with the meringues and serve.

2 egg whites

115g/4oz/½ cup soft light brown sugar, reserving 5ml/1 tsp for the peaches

pinch of ground cinnamon

6 ripe peaches, or nectarines

COOK'S TIP *The meringues can be stored in an airtight container for about 2 weeks. Serve them after dinner with coffee or with desserts in place of biscuits (cookies).*

Summer Berries in a Creamy Glaze

This luxurious combination of summer berries under a light and fluffy liqueur sauce is lightly grilled to form a crisp, caramelized topping. Fresh or frozen berries can be used in this dessert. If you use frozen berries, defrost them in a sieve over a bowl to allow the juices to drip. Stir a little juice into the fruit before dividing among the dishes.

SERVES FOUR

1 Arrange the mixed summer berries or soft fruit in four individual flameproof dishes. Preheat the grill (broiler).

2 Whisk the yolks in a large bowl with the sugar and liqueur or wine. Place over a pan of hot water and whisk constantly until the mixture is thick, fluffy and pale.

3 Pour equal quantities of the yolk mixture into each dish. Place under the grill for 1–2 minutes, until just turning brown. Add an extra splash of liqueur, if you like, and serve immediately.

450g/1lb/4 cups summer berries

4 egg yolks

50g/2oz/¼ cup vanilla sugar or caster (superfine) sugar

120ml/4fl oz/½ cup liqueur, such as Kirsch

Baked Blueberry and Almond Tart

This is a cheat's version of a frangipane tart and the result is superb. Whisked egg whites and grated marzipan cook to form a light sponge under a tangy topping of contrasting blueberries. When whisking the egg whites for the filling, ensure all traces of yolk are removed – otherwise you won't be able to achieve maximum volume.

SERVES SIX

250g/9oz (unsweetened) shortcrust pastry

175g/6oz/ generous 1 cup white marzipan

4 large (US extra large) egg whites

130g/4½oz/ generous 1 cup blueberries

1 Preheat the oven to 200°C/400°F/Gas 6. Roll out the pastry and use to line a 23cm/9in round, loose-based flan tin or quiche pan. Line with greaseproof or waxed paper and fill with baking beans, then bake for 15 minutes. Remove the beans and greaseproof paper and bake for a further 5 minutes. Reduce the oven temperature to 180°C/350°F/Gas 4.

2 Grate the marzipan. Whisk the egg whites until stiff. Sprinkle half the marzipan over them and fold in. Then fold in the rest.

3 Turn the mixture into the pastry case or pie shell and spread it evenly. Sprinkle the blueberries over the top and bake for 20–25 minutes, until golden and just set. Leave to cool for 10 minutes before serving.

Hot Chocolate and Rum Soufflés

Light as air, melt-in-the-mouth soufflés are always impressive, yet they are often based on the simplest store-cupboard ingredients. Serve them as soon as they are cooked for a fantastic finale to a special dinner party. For an extra indulgent touch, serve the soufflés with whipped cream flavoured with dark rum and grated orange rind.

SERVES SIX

50g/2oz/½ cup (unsweetened) cocoa powder

65g/2½oz/ 5 tbsp caster (superfine) sugar, plus extra caster or icing (confectioners') sugar for dusting

30ml/2 tbsp dark rum

6 egg whites

1 Preheat the oven to 190°C/375°F/Gas 3. Place a baking sheet in the oven to heat up.

2 Mix 15ml/1 tbsp of the cocoa with 15ml/1 tbsp of the sugar in a bowl. Grease six 250ml/8fl oz/1 cup ramekins. Pour the cocoa and sugar mixture into each of the dishes in turn, rotating them to coat evenly. Mix the remaining cocoa powder with the dark rum.

3 Whisk the egg whites in a clean, grease-free bowl until they form stiff peaks. Whisk in the remaining sugar. Stir a generous spoonful of the whites into the cocoa mixture to lighten, then fold in the remaining.

4 Divide the mixture among the dishes. Place on the hot baking sheet, and bake for 13–15 minutes until risen. Dust with icing sugar before serving.

Easy Bread Rolls

These soft, spongy bread rolls are irresistible while still warm and aromatic. Made with milk, rather than the more usual water, they have a rich flavour. In Scotland they are a firm favourite for breakfast with fried eggs and bacon. To speed up the rising time, place the rolls in the airing cupboard or on the top of the preheated oven.

MAKES TEN ROLLS

1 Grease two baking sheets. Sift the flour and salt together into a large bowl and make a well in the centre. Mix the yeast with the milk, then mix in 150ml/¼ pint/⅔ cup lukewarm water. Add to the centre of the flour and mix together to form a soft dough.

2 Knead the dough lightly in the bowl, then cover with lightly oiled clear film (plastic wrap) and leave to rise in a warm place for 1 hour, or until doubled in bulk. Turn the dough out on to a lightly floured surface and knock back (punch down).

3 Divide the dough into ten equal pieces. Knead lightly and, using a rolling pin, shape each piece of dough into a flat oval 10 x 7.5cm/4 x 3in, or a flat round 9cm/3½in.

4 Transfer to the prepared baking sheets, spaced well apart, and cover the rolls with oiled clear film. Leave to rise, in a warm place, for about 30 minutes.

5 Meanwhile, preheat the oven to 200°C/400°F/Gas 6. Press each roll in the centre with the three middle fingers to equalize the air bubbles and to help prevent blistering. Brush with milk and dust with flour. Bake for 15–20 minutes, or until lightly browned. Dust with more flour and cool slightly on a wire rack. Serve warm.

450g/1lb/4 cups unbleached strong white bread flour, plus extra for dusting

10ml/2 tsp salt

20g/¾oz fresh yeast

150ml/¼ pint/⅔ cup lukewarm milk, plus extra for glazing

Olive Oil Rolls

Italian-style dough, enriched and flavoured with extra virgin olive oil, is versatile for making decorative rolls. Children will love helping to make and shape these rolls into twists, fingers or any shape they want. The rolls are sure to disappear as soon as they are cool enough to eat.

MAKES SIXTEEN ROLLS

450g/1lb/4 cups strong white bread flour

10ml/2 tsp salt

15g/½oz fresh yeast

60ml/4 tbsp extra virgin olive oil, plus extra for brushing

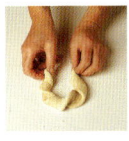

1 Lightly oil three baking sheets. Sift the flour and salt together in a large bowl and make a well in the centre. Measure 250ml/8fl oz/1 cup lukewarm water. Cream the yeast with half the water, then stir in the remainder. Add to the well with the oil and mix to a dough. Turn the dough out on to a lightly floured surface.

2 Knead for 8–10 minutes, until smooth and elastic. Place in a lightly oiled bowl, cover with lightly oiled plastic wrap and leave to rise in a warm place for about 1 hour, or until nearly doubled in bulk.

3 Knock back (punch down) the dough and divide into 12 equal pieces. To make twists, roll each piece of dough into a strip 30cm/12in long and 4cm/1½in wide. Twist each strip into a loose spiral and join the ends together to make a circle. Place on the baking sheets, spaced well apart. Brush lightly with olive oil, cover with lightly oiled clear film and leave to rise in a warm place for 20–30 minutes.

4 To make fingers, flatten each piece of dough into an oval and roll to about 23cm/9in long. Roll up from the wider end. Gently stretch the dough roll to 20–23cm/8–9in long. Cut in half. Place on the baking sheets, spaced well apart. Brush the dough with olive oil, cover with lightly oiled clear film and leave to rise in a warm place for 20–30 minutes.

5 To make artichoke-shapes, shape each piece of dough into a ball and space well apart on the baking sheets. Brush with oil, cover with lightly oiled clear film and leave to rise in a warm place for 20–30 minutes. Using scissors, snip 5mm/¼in deep cuts in a circle on the top of each ball, then make five larger horizontal cuts around the sides.

6 Preheat the oven to 200°C/400°F/Gas 6. Bake the rolls for 15 minutes. Cool on a wire rack for 20 minutes before eating.

Pitta Breads

Soft, slightly bubbly pitta bread is a pleasure to make. It can be eaten in a variety of ways, such as Mediterranean-style filled with salad or little chunks of meat cooked on the barbecue, or it can be torn into pieces and dipped in savoury dips such as hummus or tzatziki. Chop any leftover bread and incorporate into the Lebanese salad *fattoush* with parsley, mint, tomatoes and cucumber.

500g/1¼lb/5 cups strong white bread flour

12.5ml/2½ tsp easy-blend (rapid-rise) dried yeast

15ml/1 tbsp salt

15ml/1 tbsp olive oil

MAKES TWELVE

1 Combine the flour, yeast and salt. Combine the oil and 250ml/8fl oz/1 cup water, then add half of the flour mixture, stirring in the same direction, until the dough is stiff. Knead in the remaining flour. Place the dough in a clean bowl, cover with a clean dishtowel and leave in a warm place for at least 30 minutes and up to 2 hours.

2 Knead the dough for 10 minutes until smooth. Lightly oil the bowl, place the dough in it, cover, and leave to rise in a warm place for about 1 hour, or until doubled in size. Divide the dough into 12 equal pieces.

3 With lightly floured hands, flatten each piece, then roll out into a round measuring about 20cm/8in and about 4mm–1cm/¼–½in thick. Keep the rolled breads covered while you make the remaining pittas.

4 Heat a heavy frying pan over a medium-high heat. When hot, lay one piece of flattened dough in the pan and cook for 15–20 seconds. Turn it over and cook the second side for about 1 minute. When large bubbles start to form on the bread, turn it over again. It should puff up.

5 Using a clean dishtowel, gently press on the bread where the bubbles have formed. Cook for a total of 3 minutes, then remove the pitta from the pan. Repeat with the remaining dough. Wrap the pitta breads in a clean dishtowel, stacking them as each one is cooked. Serve the pittas hot while they are soft and moist.

VARIATION To bake the breads, preheat the oven to 220°C/425°F/Gas 7. Fill an unglazed or partially glazed dish with hot water and place in the bottom of the hot oven. Place a lightly oiled baking sheet in the oven for a few minutes. Place two or three pieces of flattened dough on to the hot baking sheet. Bake for 2–3 minutes until puffed up. Repeat with the remaining dough rounds.

Tandoori Breads

Indian flat breads are fun to make at home: these may not be strictly authentic in terms of cooking method, but they taste fantastic. This bread would normally be baked in a tandoor, a clay oven that is heated with charcoal. The oven becomes very hot, cooking the bread in minutes. The rotis are ready when light brown bubbles appear on the surface.

MAKES SIX ROTIS

350g/12oz/ 3 cups atta or fine wholemeal (whole-wheat) flour

5ml/1 tsp salt

30–45ml/2–3 tbsp melted ghee or butter, for brushing

1 Sift the flour and salt into a large bowl. Add 250ml/ 8fl oz/1 cup water and mix to a soft dough. Knead on a lightly floured surface for 3–4 minutes, until smooth. Place the dough in a lightly oiled mixing bowl, cover with lightly oiled plastic wrap and leave for 1 hour.

2 Turn out on to a lightly floured surface. Divide the dough into six pieces and shape each piece into a ball. Press out into a larger round with the palm of your hand, cover with lightly oiled plastic wrap and leave to rest for 10 minutes.

3 Meanwhile, preheat the oven to 230°C/450°F/Gas 8. Place three baking sheets in the oven to heat. Roll the breads into 15cm/6in rounds, place two on each baking sheet and bake for 8–10 minutes. Brush with ghee or butter and serve warm.

Index

Apple shiner, 10
Avocado soup with coriander, 16
Baby squash stuffed with cheese and rice, 42
Bacon and broad bean risotto, 49
Baked blueberry and almond tart, 58
Baked caramel custard, 54
Baked salmon with green sauce, 27
Beef patties with onions and peppers, 32
Beef stock, 6
Blackberry ice cream, 51
Bouquet garni, 7
Butter bean, sun-dried tomato and pesto soup, 18
Chicken escalopes with lemon slices and ham, 38
Chicken stock, 6
Chopped egg and onions, 22
Citrus sparkle, 11
Coconut and lime ice, 50
Crab and cucumber wraps, 29
Duck with plum sauce, 41
Easy bread rolls, 60
Feta cheese with green olives, 22
Fettucine with Parmesan and cream, 46
Filo-wrapped fish, 25
Fish stock, 7
Flavoured oils, 9
Freezing stock, 7
Fresh tomato sauce, 8
Frothy hot chocolate, 15
Fruity lamb, 34
Grilled peaches with meringues, 56
Haddock with fennel butter, 28
Hollandaise sauce, 9
Hot chocolate and rum soufflés, 59
Introduction, 4
Lamb steaks with redcurrant glaze, 35
Leek and potato soup, 17
Making basic savoury sauces, 8
Making basic stocks, 6
Mango zinger, 11
Mayonnaise, 9
Melon pick-me-up, 10
Mushroom caviar, 20
Olive oil rolls, 61
Paprika pork, 36
Pitta breads, 62
Poached fish in spicy tomato sauce, 24
Pork kebabs, 37
Prawn and new potato stew, 31
Raspberry and orange smoothie, 12
Risotto with borlotti beans, 48
Roast chicken with chilli and lime stuffing, 39
Roasted peppers with halloumi and pine nuts, 43
Scallops with fennel and bacon, 30
Soy-marinated chicken, 40
Spicy chickpea samosas, 44
Steak with warm tomato salsa, 33
Stilton and watercress soup, 19
Strawberry and banana smoothie, 12
Summer berries and meringue gateau, 53
Summer berries in a creamy glaze, 57
Tagliatelle with vegetable ribbons, 47
Tandoori breads, 63
Tofu and pepper kebabs, 45
Vanilla and Chocolate latte, 14
Vegetable stock, 7
Walnut and goat's cheese toasts, 21
White chocolate and brownie torte, 52
White sauce, 8

This edition is published by Lorenz Books,
an imprint of Anness Publishing Ltd,
108 Great Russell Street, London WC1B 3NA info@anness.com
www.annesspublishing.com; twitter: @Anness_Books

© Anness Publishing Limited 2015

If you like the images in this book and would like to investigate using them for publishing, promotions or advertising, please visit our website www.practicalpictures.com for more information.

Publisher: Joanna Lorenz
Editor: Valerie Ferguson & Helen Sudell
Production Controller: Pirong Wang

Recipes contributed by: Alex Barker, Jacqueline Clark, Joanna Farrow, Brian Glover, Jane Milton, Jennie Shapter, Marlena Spieler, Kate Whiteman.

Photography: Tim Auty, Martin Brigdale, Nicky Dowey, Gus Filgate, Michelle Garret, Amanda Heywood, William Lingwood, Craig Robertson, Simon Smith.

A CIP catalogue record for this book is available from the British Library

PUBLISHER'S NOTE:
Although the advice and information in this book are believed to be accurate and true at the time of going to press, neither the authors nor the publisher can accept any legal responsibility or liability for any errors or omissions that may have been made nor for any inaccuracies nor for any loss, harm or injury that comes about from following instructions or advice in this book.

Cook's Notes

Bracketed terms are intended for American readers.

For all recipes, quantities are given in both metric and imperial measures and, where appropriate, in standard cups and spoons. Follow one set of measures, but not a mixture.

Standard spoon and cup measures are level. 1 tsp = 5ml, 1 tbsp = 15ml, 1 cup = 250ml/ 8fl oz. Australian standard tablespoons are 20ml. Australian readers should use 3 tsp in place of 1 tbsp for measuring small quantities.

American pints are 16fl oz/2 cups. American readers should use 20fl oz/2.5 cups in place of pint when measuring liquids.

Electric oven temperatures in this book are for conventional ovens. When using a fan oven, the temperature will probably need to be reduced by about 10–20°C/20–40°F. Check with your manufacturer's instruction book for guidance.

Medium (US large) eggs are used unless otherwise stated.